Handbag Book of Girly Emergencies

First published in 2001

15 17 19 20 18 16

First published in the United Kingdom in 2001 by Vermilion
an imprint of Ebury Press
Random House
20 Vauxhall Bridge Road · London SW1V 2SA

Random House Australia (Pty) Limited
20 Alfred Street · Milsons Point · Sydney · New South Wales 2061 · Australia

Random House New Zealand Limited
18 Poland Road · Glenfield · Auckland 10 · New Zealand

Random House South Africa (Pty) Limited
Endulini · 5A Jubilee Road · Parktown 2193 · South Africa

Random House UK Limited Reg. No. 954009

Papers used by Vermilion are natural, recyclable products made from wood grown in sustainable forests.

A CIP catalogue record for this book is available from the British Library.

ISBN 0 09 188227 3

Designed by Lovelock & Co.

Printed and bound in Great Britain

the Handbag Book of Girly Emergencies

Vermilion

LONDON

The author is a white-wine swilling girly whose social life is all too frequently interrupted by the demands of her job as a journalist. Her job and a teenage stint in the army cadets, have equipped her with all sorts of essential survival techniques — not least deflecting full-frontal attacks, poorly executed night exercises and learning how to conceal a hairdryer in her ration pack. Nowadays she is more frequently seen clutching her bag in nightclubs or blagging her way into freebie parties and then trying to function at work with a hangover.

With special thanks to the wine-swilling women who always get through girly emergencies with style: Anne, Bron, Kate, Lee, Leeanne, Nicola, Paula and Shona. And with special thanks to Bobbi and Joni for those red-hot sex tips.

Contents

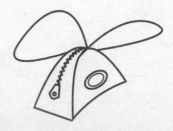

Sometimes we need a little help to *get us through* – especially if we don't have an older sister, or experienced friend to help with sticky situations.

In the Handbag Book of Girly Emergencies you'll find advice, hints and tips to *see you through* – including how to be a beach babe; beauty secrets to make you really sparkle; staying out all night in style and intimate advice on coping with eavesdropping flatmates and squeaky beds.

There is some serious stuff here too – mainly on staying healthy – but it is all done in handbag girly style so that you don't have to stop having fun to look and feel good. Enjoy!

Sex and Relationships

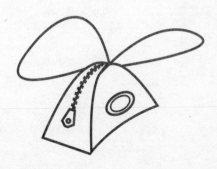

We're going to take you on a ride through some of the possible boy dilemmas a girly might face as a single girl or in a relationship. Let's start with how to find a man.

How to survive a blind date

Do
- go with a light-hearted approach
- have a laugh — make it a double date or a group situation so it won't be so awkward
- arrange to meet your mates the next day so you can have a laugh if it was bad, boast if he was gorgeous.

Don't
- assume you'll meet the man of your dreams
- feel you have to see him again if he asks
- be put off if it was a disaster — try again.

> ### *Handy love hint*
> The best way to get the attention of someone you fancy? It's simple: be really friendly when you do see or talk to them, but don't pay them too much attention and have them wondering why … uncertainty is the best aphrodisiac in the world.

On line dating

There are lots of internet dating services and some of them are free. Have a peek at some of the ads – its always a laugh and you might find someone you fancy the sound of.

Girly website

We hope you won't *ever* need it but if you do – 'soyouvebeendumped.com' is packed with wicked advice for getting over him.

Help, I feel like I never meet interesting men ...

Keep your options wide open

Don't miss out on someone gorgeous just because you are always looking in the same place. Try an older or a younger man for a bit of fun and variety.

Older men are fascinated by younger women because they hanker over what they've lost — a firm, sexy body — and they love the chance to play cool and sophisticated and splash a bit of cash. For younger men, there's nothing like the allure of a confident older woman who is experienced in every way — especially sex — and comfortable with her body.

Now you can't assume that all younger men are bimbos and that older men are suave, sophisticated and mature, but a little bit of stereotyping can be useful. So go on, you could do a lot worse than to try these tips to meet a guy of the age you desire.

How to find a younger man

Think back to all the things you used to do five or so years ago – clubbing, gigs, you name it – and go back and do them all again. Find out what music is hip and, perhaps more crucially, what isn't.

One of the places you can usually rely on to meet people of all ages is work – make friends with the younger girls in the office, take up their invitations to house parties and the pub to check out their friends. As the 'older' woman, you'll seem endlessly fascinating and experienced.

Younger man

Pros

- Sexy, firm, fit body
- Fewer hang-ups; fewer bad relationships to be scarred from
- You can enjoy looking at his mates too ...
- Open to instruction from the sexually experienced older woman (that's you, silly!).

Cons

- Sexually inexperienced?
- No money
- Smelly flat and flatmates always hanging around
- You might get insecure about younger women around him.

How to find an older man

Our advice is to forget clubs and mad bars — try some more sophisticated bars and members' clubs. Bone up on your current affairs if you aren't in touch. Accept dinner party invitations from older friends and people at work.

It might sound clichéd but it works — try galleries and bookshops, cafés and quieter winebars. As the younger woman you'll seem hip, trendy and full of life.

Girly brownie points

If you hate his mother or best friend, as much as you might want to scream at the very thought of them, keep it to yourself and restrict your rantings to moaning with your mates.

Older men

Pros

- Sexually experienced – you hope …
- Often richer and more successful
- Because of the above, more likely to have their own home(s), cars and money to lavish on you
- More confident, self assured – they've been through that twenties angst already
- You're the 'nubile young thing'.

Cons

- Baggage: ex-wives, weird pasts
- They might not wear their age well
- Nothing in common with your friends or with you out of bed …

Girly guide to pulling effortlessly

* Spend ages making yourself look gorgeous, but wear your worst knickers, then you're bound to pull.

* Go out with a friend who really makes you laugh (it helps if you're both the same number on the looks scale).

* Pick a bar that is teeming with gorgeous men.

* Get your drinks and sit somewhere central and very visible.

* Drink enough to have fun, but don't get paralytic.

* Don't look around the room until you've been there at least half an hour. Joke, laugh, look animated …

* Scan the room, catch a few eyes here and there – smile fleetingly.

▶ Go back to talking to your mate — giving off mixed vibes. You're interested in who's there but you are having fun anyway.

▶ Look surprised but moderately pleased if someone you fancy comes over to talk to you.

▶ Sit back, don't try too hard to impress, relax and enjoy the attention, you've pulled!

Girly 3-smile attack tip
Catch his eye, smile. Look away, then back again, smile — away. On the third smile he should either come over or you should give up on him and re-scan the room for another target.

Help, he hasn't called …

According to dating agencies fewer than half of first dates will lead to a second date. So here are some tips on how to get him to call:

Don't
- talk about your problems, especially your ex-boyfriend!
- brag about your sexual conquests
- have sex – wait until you've worked out whether he's worth it or a waste of space.

Do
- be a good listener and be interested in him
- relax and don't pin all your hopes on it working out
- look deep into his eyes (practise on your mates first so you look intrigued rather than mad)
- avoid getting pissed.

How to date two men at once

The key is busyness – blame it on work, pressure and trips away but let them think you're hardly ever free and they won't expect you always to be available, leaving you free to see the other guy. This way lying will be less necessary.

» Let one in on the secret – usually the one who came last. That way you're only really having to lie to one of them. And the one who 'knows' will feel you'd really like to be with him but …

» Be fair: don't declare undying love to them, use the 'I just want to have fun and not get heavy' line.

» Don't tell mates you can't trust – they'll be so jealous they'll be dying to blow your cover and tell on you.

How to avoid detection

- Have rock-solid alibis — it's best to choose non-mutual, slightly mysterious 'friends' or work contacts.
- Don't make traceable phone calls — especially if you live with your partner — and watch out for the give-away text message.
- Be careful of emails if your boyfriend has access to your computer.
- Don't leave receipts or matchboxes from restaurants in your purse where he can find them.

Super-selfish girly sex tip

Every healthily sexed-up girl should keep a running sex tally — if he came first last time then it's your turn this time; if he fell asleep before you came — get your own back by falling into a deep sleep right after you come …

What to do if you get caught

Want to keep your boyfriend?
- If you want to keep going: brazen it out, never ever admit it and if you do break down and say it was only the once.
- Say it made you realise how lucky you are to have him — *he* wasn't half as nice or good in bed …

Had enough of double lust?
- If you really are feeling the effects of such a hectic love life, admit it, be suitably apologetic and let him dump you.

Super-selfish survival tip
Don't stop seeing your friends when you fall in lust — you'll need them to pick up the pieces when it all ends in tears.

How to tell if he is seeing someone else

Look out for the signs listed previously (but less subtle as he is a bloke).

He probably *is* if:

* he seems nervous if you turn up at his flat unannounced
* he is often busy and doesn't say where he's been
* he doesn't introduce you to his friends or family
* he doesn't take you to the places he goes to with the boys
* he doesn't want sex every time, when he was always gagging for it in the past
* he has a sudden increase in work commitments or 'new' friends
* he seems more distracted than usual – or just acting out of character generally, even if doing unusually 'nice' things.

If your bloke is crap at sex
You don't have to be honest and tell him — too hard! And it opens up too many insecurities.

Be more enthusiastic about the stuff he does well to get him to do it more, and gently guide him with the stuff he does badly.

When you hate your best friend's boyfriend
Don't tell her until she's going out with the next bloke — then get it off your chest …

I always go in head first and scare men off!

Overeagerness can put men off. Think about it, if you make a new friend you don't obsess about them pursuing them relentlessly – ringing them twice a day and suggesting moving in together after only a few months – so treat love relationships in the same way. If you think you've been overeager, compensate by *not* returning his call, or standing back slightly. Don't ring him every day or always be available – pace yourself.

Essential girly website

A fab new website: boyfriends-gonebad.com – includes a list of Boyfriendsgonebad cocktails such as the 'Singleton Slurp' and a swap shop for the cappucino maker or Tiffany necklace he bought you.

I'm unlucky in love . . .

Some girly rules for not getting hurt:

- Assume nothing – just because he sleeps with you it doesn't mean he wants to be your boyfriend. He might be playing the field.
- Don't get in too deep too soon – you're bound to get hurt if you always sleep with a guy after only a date or two, getting intimate before you know him.
- Don't start banging on about commitment after the first couple of months. Need we say more: it's boring ...
- Be picky – don't assume every guy you meet is 'the one' or you'll set yourself up for disappointment.

I've just started sleeping with someone and seem to have an infection

This doesn't necessarily mean anything more than you're getting used to someone else's microbes . . . cystitis for instance is common with new partners, not least because you're usually going hell for leather. But you must get checked out by a doctor promptly. And keep using the condoms . . .

Girly morning-after tip

Keep a little packet of mints in bedside cabinet – great for getting rid of that morning breath. Offer him one, too, before you take up where you left off last night . . .

Escape scenarios

How blow out a crap date

Here's the plan:

A quick visit to the loo, ring your mate and fill her in on the situation and get her to call back with an 'emergency'. If it is really bad – like he is worryingly weird and not just boring you to death – get your mate to drop by 'accidentally' where you are and join the two of you. Her job is to drink loads of vodka, pretend to be seriously pissed and confess a recent upset and the need to be escorted home by you, alone …

Getting caught in the act

If visitors call during the day when you're in bed with a man, don your worst dressing gown, grab some tissues, put on some Vicks for smelly effect and pretend you're really ill and need to go back to bed – that'll send them packing from the front door.

How to avoid sex politely but firmly ...

When it is heading that way don't muck about, just make your excuses and leave. If you are too wimpy to say you don't fancy him, you can always pretend to be born again and saving yourself for marriage. Failing that you could look perturbed (calling on your acting skills again) and checking your pink bits say 'I've never had any cold sores or herpes but I've got this funny little spot here...' If all else fails, pretend to pass out drunk before he kisses you.

You're about to fulfil his ultimate wish when ...

Giving him a blow job that is, but then you notice that he ain't as sweet smelling as he could be. Unless you want to tell him (only worth it if he is a boyfriend you want to keep), the best thing is to shriek and feign cramp in your leg, stomp around the room clutching your leg and make such a fuss that sex is completely forgotten.

Girly flatshare sex

Sometimes it's hard enough trying to get on with flatmates without them also knowing the ins and outs of your entire life. And we mean ins and outs …unless you want your flatmates snorting and sniggering with laughter whenever you have sex because they can hear your bed squeaking take action now:

First get on the bed and have a romp — for DIY purposes of course — and listen for where the squeaking is coming from

Next If you have a wooden-framed bed which creaks, sprinkle talcum powder into the joints — get a little paintbrush and really push it into the gaps. If you have a spring mattress bed put some cooking oil on a paintbrush and paint oil on to the squeaky bits — also works for squeaky doors if you live or stay with your parents and don't want them to hear you coming in at dawn.

If this advice fails, get out of bed and carry on doing it on the floor — bed is boring anyway.

If you really want to look good in bed – fake it

- At bedtime assume the missionary position – the flesh on your stomach will flatten out, hiding your pot belly.
- If your belly is fine but your breasts are small get on top, they'll look bigger from where he's lying.
- Discover the wonders of discreet or low-level lighting or candles on the floor or around the bed. They are much more flattering than stark mega-watt overhead lighting.

Girly satisfaction

Buy for yourself and carry at all times an Ann Summers lipstick vibrator – no one will ever know what it really is and what you get up to with it, and you never know when you might need it.

We've just hit the 6-month mark – how do we keep the passion going?

We could go on for ages about sex toys, but the simple rule is that you have to have sex even when you're knackered – if you'd said no when you were tired when you were first going out, you'd never have had those brilliantly acrobatic, all-night sessions, would you?

Passion boosters:
- Keep on doing it outside the bedroom.
- Avoid that once-at-the-weekend shag routine.
- Take the lead, don't make him do it all the time.
- Try new things, don't just stick to trusty favourites.
- Make an effort to go away on romantic weekends à deux so you get to spend extra time in bed.

'Aaagh – I've just been dumped'

It is possible to emerge smiling from a traumatic dumping –
honestly!

> Scream. Get it out of your system. Don't sink into a pit of
> self-pity. Think positive!

> Don't lock yourself away and bury your head in the
> sand ... keeping busy helps the healing process. Arrange
> lots of nights out, catch up with people you haven't seen
> because you've been too busy with HIM. Make plans for
> the future too. Keeping the broader picture in mind will
> stop you feeling so panicked.

> Spend £££s on your appearance to look better and sexier
> than you have in ages.

- Do all the stuff you stopped doing because he didn't like doing it. Sweat it all out down at the gym or pamper yourself with beauty treatments.

- Wear those high heels that made you tower over him (like Nicole Kidman after her divorce from Tom Cruise) or that revealing dress that drove him crazy because other blokes were looking at you.

- Have fun and remember all those good things about being single. Go out with single friends and allow yourself to ogle men unashamedly and wink whenever you dare.

- Get into something new — whether job, hobby, DIY, going out with new group of friends or colleagues.

How can I dump him without being a bitch?

Much as you're tempted to cut him loose so that you can get onto the next bloke ... try to be a little bit caring about it before you shelve him and run off to find someone new:

- Forget personal reasons. Use the old cliché, 'It's not you that's the problem, it's me ...' Blaming yourself will make him feel better and get it over more quickly.
- Make it gentle but also keep it short. Try to be as honest as possible without letting him know it's something physical or an emotional problem with him. For example:
  - 'You're a great bloke, but I'm not sure it's a long-term thing.'
  - or: 'I care about you too much to lead you on.'
  - or: 'It just doesn't feel right.'
- Don't give him false hopes that you might change your mind – make a clean break and be clear with your message.

I need to wangle my way out of my relationship, fast!

The easiest way is to say that you have to go to Australia — next week — to sort out a family problem. The only catch is that you'll have to lie low and stay away from your usual haunts for a while.

OR

If you're really feeling desperate and cruel (like a friend of ours), just never take his calls again. It will slowly and painfully sink in.

Lifestyle

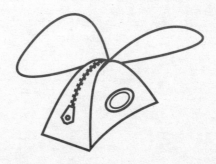

The girly guide to a balanced lifestyle

It's great fun partying non-stop but it can be knackering too and we all need time to recover. We're not going to tell you to stop doing naughty things — NO WAY — well, you wouldn't anyway would you? The girly motto is 'don't stop, find an antidote'. We're not saying give up drinking and spend every hour in the gym but for every bad thing you do, you then do something 'good' to compensate and then you needn't worry at all. Your conscience will be clear.

Typical girly excesses	**The girly antidote**
Lots of booze, partying and generally living to the max	Eat more liver-boosting foods (see p184) Have the odd weekend in – when you're skint is a good time …
Loadsa fags	You need to take a good vitamin C supplement regularly.
	If you've tried giving up only to fail try this method: look out for older women who smoke – zoom in on their mouths – those lines around their lips are puffing lines from drawing on a cigarette. Note also their grey skin – also down to the fags. Not a good look girls.

Typical girly excesses	The girly antidote
Croissants and doughnuts everyday	To curb your cravings, visualise your bottom growing in size every time you eat them.

Go for muesli and fruit, a smoothie or porridge instead – at least every other day. |
| Crazy clubbing nights | Take a good multivitamin.

Go out with your dullest friend who can't dance to save her life – you'll be dying to get away for an early night. |

Typical girly excesses	**The girly antidote**
A new man – night after night of rampant sex	You want to be able to keep it up, don't, you so: ▶ make sure you keep taking that multivitamin ▶ have KY jelly on hand to lubricate and stop soreness from friction ▶ always have a pee after sex to ward off cystitis.
Stressed-out at work	Occasionally have some therapy by hanging around the photocopier or water fountain and gossip with everyone who comes by … Surf the internet – use a search engine to avoid detection.

I'm having trouble sleeping...

One in three of us is affected by insomnia at some time in our life – due to stress, depression, difficulties at work, relationship troubles, too many stimulants or eating too late at night.

- Try cutting back on anything containing caffeine, including chocolate, cola, tea and coffee. Alcohol is a sleep-killer too – unless you've had so many you pass out, though you won't really be getting quality sleep that way.
- Relax mentally and slow down: read, listen to relaxing music or have a relaxing bath.
- Go to bed at roughly the same time each evening. Your body gets into a routine.
- Try chamomile tea, and herbal sleeping pills. Or try writing down all your worries at least an hour before you go to bed.
- If all else fails, have sex, it works wonders to knock you out by releasing endorphins.

DIY emergency one-minute facial massage

Done regularly it will boost your circulation and keep your skin bright and glowing.

Using your cleanser on moist skin, massage your face in small circular movements along your jaw-line from your ear to your chin.

Smooth your fingertips in a large circle up from your chin, past the outer corners of your mouth, along the sides of your nose and past the inner corners of your eyes to your temples, then back down the sides of your face to your chin.

Work in light circles around your eyes, sweeping over your eyebrows. Then press lightly and evenly with your two middle fingers along your cheekbones to your nose and up to the bridge of your nose.

Help, I'm panicking when I really need to appear cool and confident

If you've got to get through something that's making you nervous you need help fast … Combat your fears by thinking of a calm and relaxing scene or a time when you felt loved, relaxed and happy. Breathe deeply and evenly and repeat over and over 'I am calm, I am calm'.

I'm going out with someone I really fancy tonight and I am stressing like mad

An hour before you go out burn some lavender oil in an oil burner, put on some super-chilled music and lie on the sofa and visualise yourself acting cool, calm and confident and having a great time.

Work worries

Job interview/asking for a pay rise

Preparation is key – you must think carefully about what you might be asked. Prepare some answers. Pre-empt any excuses by thinking up the solutions and incorporating them into your argument. If you want a pay rise think about why it is justified and why you've worth it! When you go in, smile, sit comfortably, not on the edge of the chair, and be enthusiastic. Speak slowly and clearly and consider what you say. Be firm but not too demanding. Good luck!

Girly calming tips
- Burn some peppermint oil to help concentration
- Wear blue to make you feel calmer and serene

Help, I can't get up in the morning

I can't face another morning having to drag myself out of bed, barely waking up before I stumble into work

In a perfect world you'd bounce out of bed ready to squeeze fresh juice and do your yoga routine. Sadly we're not all made that way, but you can give yourself a kick-start by doing some duvet-stretches when you wake up – sounds obvious but you'll be amazed at how good it makes you feel and, after all, how hard can it be to do a bit of stretching when you're still in bed?

While you're still in bed: Screw up your face and say 'wow' in a really exaggerated way using all of your facial muscles (be warned that any nearby males will probably think you're talking about them). Stretch your arms above your head – stretching right into your fingertips and give a big yawn.

Dragging yourself up: Now get out of bed and point your toes. Then shake your legs and do just a couple of star jumps. Or if you really want to wake up grab a skipping rope and skip for a few minutes or dance around to the radio – it'll raise your heart rate, give you an energy boost and a healthy glow that will last for hours – not to mention the possibility of burning 300-660 calories an hour depending on how fast you skip.

Get fresh: Now you're ready for the shower. Grab a handful of sea salt to give yourself a quick, invigorating wake-up scrub – as gently or as stimulating as you like. Keep a huge glass of water in your bedroom so that you can start getting in your daily buckets of H_2O while you're getting dressed.

Did you know? Doing some simple stretches every day is thought to help alleviate conditions such as asthma; and bronchial, stomach, period and bowel problems.

If I'm late for work once more I'll get the sack

If you're really crap at getting out of bed try this foolproof method for getting up. Buy three alarm clocks with loud bells. Set one next to your bed for the time you want to get up. Set another at your bedroom door for five minutes later and another outside your door leading to the bathroom. They'll drive you (and whoever you live with) so crazy you'll be up and out of bed to switch them off before you know it.

Take a one-minute meditation

When you really feel that things are coming down on you — be it work or a tense scene with your man … Find a quiet place and make yourself comfortable. Close your eyes and concentrate on your in and out breath. First let your belly expand as it fills with air and then watch your chest fill and rise. When you exhale, empty out from the chest first and then the belly. Repeat this until you feel calmer and more focused — it shouldn't take long.

Girly mental health

Got the blues and think you need some help? Don't panic and give yourself a hard time when you are feeling sad and don't always 'run away' by going out on the piss. Sometimes you just need to let yourself feel what you feel without trying to shake yourself out of it. Don't deny your feelings, they'll always resurface anyway.

Signs that you may be depressed:
- trouble sleeping
- avoiding your friends
- loss of appetite
- loss of sex drive
- skiving off work
- suddenly becoming argumentative or listless without putting your finger on why.

Things that help:

- a brisk walk or any exercise at all
- talking to your friends or a counsellor
- seeing your doctor
- keeping a journal, write down all your worries
- St John's Wort — an antidepressant herb. Books can also help, try your local bookshop.

Girly Get-up-and-go tip

Another tip to kick-start your system in the morning is a detox drink of lemon juice, olive oil and hot water. This drink will stimulate the flow of bile which in turn helps to digests food.

Combine:
- a teaspoon of olive oil
- the juice of a lemon
- top up with boiling water
- drink and feel healthy

I've only got a tenner and there is still a week to go before payday ...

Don't stay home and get depressed or ignore your empty purse and keep spending on your credit card.

- Go to any freebie event you can at work — leaving drinks and parties.

- Sex is free for girls — ring your favourite man and tell him that you're naked and you really feel like him, chocolate and wine in bed, can he sort it for you ...

- Go man hunting — cruise the supermarket, the video store, wine shops, the street, the park.

❧ You can sit for hours in a café for the price of a coffee — take a book, read their papers or just watch other people.

❧ Visit your mates who you know to have well-stocked fridges.

❧ Only go shopping after the shops have closed — peer through the windows and plan what to buy when you get paid.

Help! ***Another rainy day – I can't face it*** …
Make a quick trip to the supermarket and have an all-day brunch. Buy fresh croissants, good coffee, papers, glossy magazines, smoked salmon for lunch or get a pizza delivery. Open the white wine when you feel like it, even if it's only 10am.

If you're stocked up with food and videos you can stay in your warm slob-out gear all day and watch some old movies.

Beauty

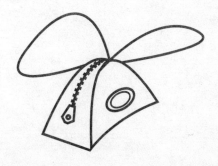

The emergency desk pack...

A must-have for when you're asked out at the last minute and want to look fab ... OR
for when you've stayed out all night and don't want the whole office to know ...

- spare, sexy pants
- push-me up and give-me-a-cleavage bra
- fuck-me shoes
- condoms
- perfume
- dry shampoo
- eye drops
- toothbrush and toothpaste
- deowipes – new fabulous babywipes for grown-ups
- sexy, strappy top
- big hoop earrings or a piece of groovy jewellery

I've just got up, I look a slob and someone's at the door

You know it's not a pizza delivery man or a Jehovah's Witness but possibly your bloke ... with only a minute available what's a girl to do?

Shout 'just a minute' and splash your face with cold water, tip your head upside-down for few seconds to get the blood into your face. Slap on some cheek and lip stain which immediately brightens your face and gives you a flushed sexy look instead of tired and scruffy. Spray on perfume. Da da!

No time for all that? Greasy hair?
Don't panic, simply wrap a towel around your head put on your best dressing gown and pretend you were in the shower.

Basic rules for fab skin

- Eat good food and drink plenty of water.
- Great circulation — from regular exercise to get blood pumping. This includes sex, girls!
- Get plenty of sleep.
- A simple but daily regime: cleanse, tone, moisturise.
- Wear sunscreen or cream with UVA protection every day.
- Give yourself a good scrub! Exfoliate once or twice a week.
- Take vitamins, especially zinc and Vitamin E.
- Give up, or cut down on smoking — you know it's not good.

The two-minute face
Use tinted moisturiser — forget foundation as it takes too long. A few strokes of bronzer across nose and cheek bones. Apply mascara and lipgloss. Run out the door.

Problems – Seasonal emergencies ...

Help, I get oily skin in summer

Lighter oil-free moisturisers will be better for you as
conditions start to heat up. Use a gentle foaming cleanser to
really clean your skin. Once again UV protection is important,
not forgetting your lips to keep them soft and moist.

I have an embarrasing sweat problem!

Again, this is something to thank your genes for, but reduce
the problem by wearing natural fibres and a good (sports or
'active' type) antiperspirant deodorant. Keep a change of
clothes handy if it makes you feel more comfortable.

Ouch, I've got sunburnt

If you have an aloe vera plant to hand (also v. good for kitchen
burns) snap off a leaf and apply it directly to the affected

skin, but equally good is the gel you can buy from the chemist. If neither of these is to be found in your holiday hotel room, or wherever you are, add vinegar to your bath instead.

I've sunbathed too much and I have a sun damage, what can I do?

If you're a good girl from now on and wear good sun protection and a daily moisturiser containing a sunscreen the skin is able to repair up to 35% of damage done in the past. Go for a moisturiser with antioxidant vitamins to try to undo the damage.

My skin gets really dry in winter

Prevent your skin from drying out and lips from chapping by wearing protective moisturisers. Use a cream cleanser which will be gentle on your skin. Take an essential oil supplement such as evening primrose oil. Taking a teaspoon of flaxseed oil morning and night will also do the trick.

How do I hide a red nose?

It sounds crazy but it is true that green tinted skin concealer
tones down rosy areas — red noses and spots — but apply it
under your normal foundation and powder.

I always get chapped lips in winter

Massage dry lips with a fingerful of Vaseline. Leave for 2
minutes then remove gently with a damp facecloth or
toothbrush. This will remove those dry, flaky bits. Always carry
around a lip balm or one of those little handy tubs of Vaseline.
Lip gloss tends to dry out lips less than lipstick.

My skin is pale and pasty after winter months

Use some light face tan for a very subtle colour. Do it at the
weekend so that you can pretend that there was a freak patch
of sunshine wherever you were. If you're unsure get some
advice at a beauty counter.

Puffy eyes and other problems

An angry zit has just popped up on my nose

Hold an ice cube over it for a few seconds. If you have any to hand apply eye drops for red eyes on a cotton bud – it has the same effect. Apply a medicated concealer – just on the spot itself, and blend round the edge with another cotton bud.

Help, my eyes are puffy

You may laugh but many top models use haemorrhoid cream to deal with puffy eyes from a bad night's sleep or too much partying. You get a great instant facelift.

Chilled out beauty tip

Refrigerate toner and foundation so that they are chilled for application – they're great for reducing facial puffiness.

Help me get rid of my nicotine-stained fingers

Bleach nicotine stains with a slice of lemon – or brush with a toothbrush and toothpaste. Apply handcream liberally afterwards. A nail buffer might also help to fade the stains.

My Rampant Red nail polish has turned my toenails yellow

Use lemon juice or white wine vinegar on a cotton bud to bleach discoloured nails.

Nail tips

For a cheap manicure: Soak fingertips in a cup of water and the juice of half a lemon for 5 mins, rinse, dry. Stick your hand in the fridge/ freezer to speed up nail drying. Keep nail polish in the fridge – it makes it smoother and easier to apply and stops separation.

I've got close-set eyes, what can I do?

Use darker eyeshadow on the outer not inner eyes. Use lighter shadow or liner – white is good – on the inner eyes.

I've had a fake-tan disaster!

Bleach orangey cuticles or elbows or any other problem areas with half a lemon. Then apply moisturiser. Alternatively use a body scrub every 10 minutes until you cant bear it anymore. Apply bronzing powder liberally to cover up any lingering stripesor if you feel confident fill in any white bits with a little fake tan.

My pores are huge, what can I do?

For an emergency 'vodka tonic' pore tightener, a small amount of vodka on cotton wool will tighten pores on the nose and chin. A slice of lemon rubbed over large pores will also tighten them. Try to stop squeezing spots which makes this worse.

I've woken up with a wart! (on my finger, not in my bed …)

Prick a Vitamin A oil capsule (from a health food shop or chemist), mix with a drop of lemon juice and dab onto wart.

How can I fix my stained, yellowy teeth?

- Use Pearl Drops.
- Make regular trips to the dentist for a scale and polish.
- Avoid black coffee and red wine.
- Use vinegar as a cheap and easy mouthwash. Use half and half with water.
- Avoid coral or brown-based lipsticks — use red or natural pinky shades which tone down yellowness.

Help, I've got scars left by spots

Prick open some Vitamin E oil capsules and apply the oil to scars before bedtime. It really helps skin heal much quicker.

I've got dark shadows under my eyes ...

Genetics or lifestyle have a lot to do with this ... you can do sod all about the former but you can deal with the causes by getting plenty of sleep and fresh air and eating plenty of fibre. There's no 100% way to remove them (though there are some very good eye gels and creams on the market as well as concealers – especially YSL Touche Éclat), but try this: soak a cotton pad in very cold water, pat on skin, dry off, then dot concealer on before your foundation. Use a very creamy one on this delicate skin.

To banish under-eye shadows:

Hold slices of raw potato to dark shadows – it contains potassium which is quite possibly what you pay for in the expensive eye gels with 'vegetable extracts'. Also eat lots of potassium-rich foods: bananas are especially good.

I've got stinky breath – how can I freshen up?

If you haven't got any mouthwash handy or you're out and about, chew on some parsley. At home you can boil some mint or try peppermint tea. Chewing on a clove can also do the trick.

I've got a cold sore, how can I stop it turning into a throbber?

Dip an aspirin in cold water then hold it on the sore for a couple of minutes. Thereafter use a coldsore cream from your chemist.

Girly's essential emergency beauty store cupboard

The ten things you should always have in the kitchen — even if you don't have the ingredients to make a proper meal:

1 Yoghurt — good for sunburn, a cheap cleanser, hangover smoothies and thrush

2 Lemons — essential for gin and tonics, detoxing, bleaching stained nails, orange elbows and DIY sun bleached hair

3 Honey — a natural healthy comfort food for adding to tea, for sore throats, or as a cheap face pack

4 Nurofen and aspirin — do we need to spell it out? Also for cold sores and green-hair disasters.

5   Teabags — for morning-after eye packs, restorative cups of tea, tearful mates at the door and other moments of trauma

6   Cucumber — for eyes, facepacks — and adding to Pimm's

7   Olive oil — for all sorts of bodily needs from bath oil to moisturiser to a healthy dressing for your salad

8   Ice cubes — a girl should always keep a stash for impromptu drinks parties, puffy eyes, spots and 9½ *Weeks'* style antics

9   Bicarbonate of soda — for smelly shoes, clothes and cystitis (see p133 Girly housekeeping tips)

10 Chocolate of course.

Girly guide to looking like a babe on a budget

We could spend huge wads of cash on beautifying products and treatments if we wanted to, but sadly most of us can't afford fifty-quid pots of face cream or weekly facials at beauty salons.

It's easy to dismiss 'home-made' stuff as naff or old-fashioned but some of the most sought-after products have been developed by mucking around in the kitchen with natural ingredients. These beauty boosts for your face and body are all inexpensive and available from the supermarket.

Girly tight-wad tip
Apply your toner to damp cotton wool otherwise it will 'drink' up all of your toner and you'll need to use more.

FACE

- Quick cleanser — to cleanse and remove dirt and make up — apply plain, live yoghurt to your skin and splash off with warm water.

- Skin tonic — warm chamomile tea is an excellent skin toner for dry, sensitive skin; rosewater (from the cake-baking aisle) is a refreshing, fragrant skin tonic and you can pour it into your bath for a rose-petal fraganced bath.

- A refreshing face mask for oily skin is a mashed cucumber spead over your face – lie back and relax for 10 minutes.

- Keep free sachets of moisturisers, foundations and hair products from magazines and samples from cosmetic counters. Use them for weekend trips or travelling, so you don't have to carry heavy bottles with you.

- Make your own cleansing grains by adding a teaspoon of brown sugar to a natural, pure soap. This can be used gently on your face or rubbed onto your body for a scrub.

- Make your own vitamin-enhanced moisturiser by splitting open Vitamin E, D or A oil capsules and adding them to a cheap and cheerful moisturiser.

DIY Botox: girly DIY plastic surgery

It's free and it doesn't involve injecting mould into your face. Botox doesn't get rid of your wrinkles it just paralyses the area so that you can't keep frowning, with the effect that the wrinkles become softer and less noticeable. Mimic the effect at home – the moment you get home at night apply some surgical tape between your eyebrows and to your forehead. You'll know when you are frowning because the tape will rumple and you can stop immediately.

* Mix together a tablespoon of oats and 2 tablespoons of hot water – gently rub onto your skin and then rinse off.

* Facial – apply organic honey to the skin, leave on for one hour then rinse off with warm water.

* A 1p face pack – boil some full-fat milk in a pan, let it go cold and skim off the skin that forms and lay it on your face. When it has dried rub into your skin, rinse off – you won't believe how soft and supple your skin will feel.

Instant facial

Mash half an avocado and spread thickly on your face. Leave on for 5 mins then rinse off with warm water.

No avocado in the fridge? Beat an egg white till foamy then leave on face till it dries. Rinse off.

MAKE-UP

- Use a little lipstick on your cheeks if you've run out of blusher – or carry it to use for both if you've limited pocket space.

- Make your own medicated concealer by adding a drop of witch hazel or tea tree oil to your foundation and dabbing it on problem areas and spots.

- Cut open plastic tubes of moisturiser, cleanser and make-up when they run dry – you'll eke it out for a few more times.

Girly tight-wad tip
Make your own tinted moisturiser by adding a few drops of your foundation to a little of your moisturiser and mixing on the back of your hand. Apply to face.

- When your mascara dries up put it in a glass of hot water to loosen it up.

- If you suddenly run out of eyeliner, dip your eyeliner brush into your mascara – this does the job just as well.

Body

- A generous splash of olive oil in bathwater is a great skin softener – but avoid the chilli variety, girls …

- If you can't afford professional pampering … grab a handful of sea salt, mix with some olive oil and rub yourself all over in the shower.

- Throw some grapefruit halves (pulp removed) in your bath for a refreshing soak.

- Sea salt in the bath mimics the beneficial effects of the ocean and makes for an invigorating dip.

- For a cheap, effective body moisturiser, massage yourself with olive oil.

- Use the (clean) avocado stone – after making the facial mask on p.76 – to rub over body.

- Add a few drops of your favourite perfume to some almond oil – or even olive oil – this is a cheap luxury scented bath.

Eyebrows

It takes 10 minutes and costs under a tenner to get a shape and wax done professionally – it's worth every penny and will really give your face a lift.

Puffy eyes and fuzzy head sorter
Put ice cubes on your eyelids for about 2 minutes. You could even stick your head in the freezer if you can take it.

Help, I've got terrible bags and red eyes ...
Keep eye drops in the bathroom cabinet. Keep an eye mask in fridge, or lie down for 10 minutes with cold teabags over your eyes.

NAILS
How can I improve my nails?
- Take vitamin D, or one of those vitamin supplements specially formulated for nails. Apply moisturising cream at night; get yourself some gorgeous Marigolds.
- Need great nails tomorrow? Get some false nails — they can be as short and discreet or as talon-like as you want.

Top tips for sexy toes and feet

Soak to soften; smooth away rough skin with a pumice stone
or special foot scrub; apply foot cream. Once a week cover
your feet with rich foot cream, and go to bed in socks —
not very sexy but it does the trick and stops embarrassment,
allowing you lie back and enjoy it when your bloke sucks
your toes.

Girly toe tips

- Use a normal bodyscrub on your feet if you haven't got any
  specially formulated footscrub.
- In a rush, no time to paint your toe-nails? Put your shoes on,
  then only paint the toes that show.

Hair

Grrr my flatmate's used up the shampoo

Another stupid-sounding idea that does actually work … use
some Fairy Liquid instead of shampoo — it's not a lot different
in composition really and it also serves to remove the build-up
caused by repeated use of various hair products.

Help, I've got dull and lifeless hair

For glossy hair, wash it every other day if possible so that it
doesn't end up too dry. Or try the high-tech serums that are
available now for instant gloss.

Girly cheap and cheerful hair hints:

- Mayonnaise (!) conditioner — slap on the Hellman's after
  washing, cover with towel or plastic bag, leave for 15 mins —
  but forget the garlic variety …

- Have a hair pack treat every couple of weeks or so. You can use shop-bought ones or hot oil under a towel.
- Wash your hairbrush regularly.
- Split ends — the only real solution is to cut off the split hair.

Hairdressing disaster 1 - and why it's sometimes good to smoke!

I've just dyed my hair with a DIY kit at home and I've got hair dye stains on my face and scalp.

Light a fag — it'll calm your nerves and you can use the ash to remove the dye. Dip a dampened cloth in the ash and rub on stained areas.

I've run out of conditioner

Sounds crazy but you can use fabric conditioner — but dilute it with an equivalent quantity of water. You'll smell like a country meadow or summer breeze but your hair will be soft.

My hair has gone green from a dip in the swimming pool …

Don't despair there are two items which a girl might have to hand — soluble aspirin and red wine.

- Dissolve ten aspirins in a jug of warm water. Pour over your hair, keeping on for 5 mins. Do the same with the wine.
- Red wine? *Really.* It's like the red spot, green concealer thing — the same principle of one cancelling out the other.

Hairdressing disaster 2

Oh my God, I've just had the worst haircut of my life — it's a disaster, I'll never be able to show my face again …

Don't compound the nightmare by tipping the bitch/bastard — if you are close to tears and can't say how awful it is just get out of there fast, and never, ever go back.

Do go straight to Claire's Accessories. It might be full of pre-teens giggling over the plastic hair bobbles but you won't bump into anyone you know and you'll be able to grab an armful of cheap and cheerful hair accessories to hide your disaster. Clips, combs and ties will all help to hide your nightmare hair.

Do tell everyone you know about your crap hairdresser to extract the maximum revenge from the situation.

Girly hair tips

- A hairdresser to the celebs tells us that if you're short of money it is better to spend it on a good shampoo than an expensive conditioner.
- Want to wear your hair up? It will go up and stay put more easily if it's not freshly washed – dirty is good!

BODY

I've got stretch marks, what can I do?

There's not a lot, bar surgery, you can do once you've got these – and they're not something only pregnant women get. Try not to get them in the first place by avoiding any rapid weight gain or loss – this can be one of the side-effects of going on a too-drastic starvation diet – and keep skin moisturised. Stretch marks do fade and the whitish lines can be disguised with fake tan.

Aargh! The dreaded dimpled cellulite has started to appear on my thighs

Hold tight – don't rush out and buy expensive buttock and thigh firming creams. Try our suggestions first – they're cheap and they work!

Skin brushing

Give yourself a dry brush before jumping into the shower —
start from the feet working up towards your heart. We use a
soft, dry flannel but you can buy skin brushes if you really
want to give yourself a good brush. Brush up from lymph
glands behind the knees and groin. You will notice a
difference after just a few days' brushing.

Exercise

Yoga, aerobics and stretching all work to stimulate a sluggish
lymph system. Even brisk walking is better than nothing.

Feast

Yes, that is what we said — on fruits, vegetables and whole
grains to get your whole system working like it ought to. Eat at
least five servings of fresh fruit and veg every day.

Detox

Reduce the toxins in your diet – caffeine, alcohol, fat, sugar and salt – boring, we know – and keep up your intake of water: a bare minimum of a litre a day is essential, a second litre if you can do it will work wonders.

Essential oils

To improve your circulation make up some massage oil for your problem bits from a base of almond oil and a few drops of these essential oils – geranium, cypress, grapefruit, lemon and rosemary.

Girly secrets – DIY cellulite cream

Add two drops each of rosemary and fennel essential oils to three teaspoons of base oil (e.g. almond). Massage into problem areas every day.

Make-up – do's and don'ts

❧ On features you're not overly fond of don't use shimmery powders or the imperfection will be highlighted – use the sparkling make-up on your good features – to draw attention away from your not-so-perfect points.

❧ Remember sponges, brushes and powder puffs harbour germs. Wash them regularly in shampoo, especially flat sponges you get in compacts which can get clogged up with powder. Rinse in shampoo; allow to dry before using.

❧ Dab on a drop of tea tree oil and use 'medicated' concealers that have an active ingredient to treat spots.

❧ Brush your eyelashes lightly with translucent powder before applying mascara – it will make them more luscious.

Tips from the pros

❧ New-wave gel or cream blushers are more youthful and
natural-looking than old-fashioned compact and shimmery
powders. Look out for those in tubes. Use only on the parts
of face which naturally blush — the 'apples' of cheeks —
rather than scary 80's-style cheekbones.

❧ Use foundation over your eyelids to make eye make-up
stick longer.

❧ For a pouty, sophisticated look, just apply a blob of clear lip
gloss on centre of top lip rather than all over.

❧ If you've got cool skin tones (pale or sallow rather than rosy
or peachy) avoid cool colours such as blue, silver and green
— these emphasise dark under-eye shadows or redness.

❧ Line eyes with a white pencil – it makes them look bigger.

❧ Light blue pencil under the eyes makes whites look brighter.

❧ Don't go for heavy, dark colour on your eyelids unless
you've got large eyes. Also, be careful of applying dark
colour near the nose or you'll look as if your eyes are too
close together.

❧ Always use an eyelash curler, but heat it with your hairdryer
first to make it even more efficient – like mini curling tongs.

❧ Blend foundation outwards and downwards so the downy
hairs on your face do not appear raised up and more
noticeable.

Going Out

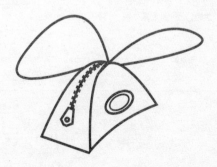

Countdown to a special event

How to be totally prepared for that big occasion

If you're anything like us you probably think months in advance about what you'll wear to a wedding or big party but sadly the finer details end up being left until the last minute. Of course we never quite get everything, or ourselves, together, having to apply make-up in the car or paint toenails on the train.

Looking gorgeous is the number one thing to sort out before going out. Whether it's an impromptu drink or a special occasion that you've spent weeks trying to find the right outfit for, here's how to avert last minute emergencies.

Top-to-toe checklist:

❧ Skin – use an instant pick-me-up radiance face pack, or try our emergency DIY ones on p.74. Most of the big cosmetics houses now do 'instant radiance' creams with minute particles that reflect light off the skin, or contain chemicals that get the blood vessels going to promote a healthy glow.

Fake tan is always a good instant fix, and there are now many powder products for instant glow and shimmer.

❧ Eyes – a great tip is to use a bit of white cream pencil or liquid liner on the inner corner of the eye to give depth and sparkle to eyes.

❧ Nails – make sure you do them the night before so you don't get smudging disasters in the rush of getting ready.

* Body — are you fully prepared for those close encounters? Think muff management, buffed body, the right underwear and sexily painted toenails.

* If you're having your legs or eyebrows waxed do it the day before you're going out — you don't want to look like a plucked chicken.

Do

Get your hair done by a known and trusted stylist. If you're getting it cut do so a week before to allow the style to settle in.

Don't

Try out any new make up techniques on the day. If you want to try something new, roadtest it beforehand.

Party gear

Now to get your clothes in order:

Pre-plan exactly what you are wearing right down to the underwear and accessories. Don't rely on being able to buy the right shoes or handbag on the day. A few days before get everything out and check it. You'll still have time for emergency dry cleaning or repairs.

Buy your undies and thongs one size bigger — they're more comfortable and they'll look better. You'll also avoid the rumply, bulgy effect as he runs his hands down your body.

The do's and don'ts of big pants

DO wear them if you want to scare a man off.
DON'T wear them if you want to look sexy. If you really are a diehard big-pants girl, buy some of those tight-fitting lycra

short-style pants — they can look really hot on the right sort of bottoms.

Disguises

Use diversionary tactics to shift attention away from your less than perfect features — if your bottom is on the large side accentuate your breasts by wearing an uplift bra and draw his attention to your cleavage so he won't notice the rest.

A basque will hold your belly in if it is not your best point. It conceals your pot or bulges and has the added bonus of being most men's idea of the ultimate in sexiness.

Top tip for big bums

Silky French knickers look and feel great and will make a larger bottom look better.

Bum – Do you have a visible panty line? Check your rear view … when you sit or bend down in your hipster trousers, does the top half of your thong reveal itself to the people sitting behind? You need to invest in some hipster thong-knickers that are available now.

Boobs – Are you wearing the right bra? Check for unseemly bulges behind the armpit, or slight spillage over the top of the cups revealed by your tight T-shirt – common signs of a bra that is slightly too small, especially at those times of PMT water retention. Check out the new moulded 'T-shirt' bras which hide perky nipples too. Does your bra strap keep showing? If so you're wearing the wrong size and you need to get yourself properly measured.

Clothing disasters

- Emergency repairs and disasters
  If your hem comes down stick it back up with Sellotape as a
  short-term measure. Use the non-crinkly stuff so you won't
  rustle and give it away.

- Monthly mishaps
  Grab a cardie and tie it around your waist – find your mate and
  get her to rinse and blow dry your trousers while you hide in
  the loo.

Static driving you crazy? Skirt riding up because of it?

- Wet your hands, apply a five-pence-piece amount of washing
  up liquid, rub your hands together and then smooth your
  tights or the inside of your skirt/dress. This eliminates
  static instantly.

OR

- Lightly spray hairspray up your skirt or inside trouser legs.

How to achive a flat stomach in three days

The last thing you need when you want to look fab is a pot belly — here's how to make sure your stomach is as flat as a pancake in three days.

Basically, you need to include certain foods and exclude others — pretty simple really — make sure you eat foods that will soothe your intestinal tract and therefore reduce any bloating and sticky-out stomach situations.

Prevent bloating by following these emergency beat-the-bloat rules:

Out

Don't touch any of these if you want a flat belly:

* dairy foods
* fizzy drinks and other things that introduce air into your system – like talking when you eat
* yeasty foods like bread and beer
* sugary foods
* starch and protein foods eaten together
* do we really have to say? – junk food of any kind
* salt – it increases water retention

In

Get stuck into these and you'll have that flat stomach in days:

- salads
- lots of vegetables – although go easy on veg like sprouts and cabbage
- fish and chicken
- fruit – eaten separately from other food
- porridge oats for soluble fibre
- live yoghurt
- peppermint oil capsules

Do:

- chew your food properly
- drink lots of still water

- If you are really desperate, give up the carbohydrates for three days, eating only fruit and vegetables. Don't do this for any longer than this unless you think looking like a pole with a too big head is a good look ...

- To ease water retention and get a flat stomach in a sexy dress, add some watercress to a salad or munch on apples, chew parsley, reduce the salt in your cooking and drink nettle tea. Not an appetising suggestion but beauty costs!

Girly one-minute yoga move

With your feet apart and your hands on your upper thighs, breathe in. Exhale fully, then push your stomach in and out ten times. Inhale, exhale fully, and repeat the move.

Staying out all night handbag kit – dont forget it!

- Condoms, contraceptive pill, toothbrush, contact lens case, sample sizes of moisturiser and perfume, make-up, deodorant wipes, peppermints, hair tie, Berocca, teeny g-string.

The next day:
- Give your skin a good scrub while in the shower, don't skimp on fragrance as boozy fumes coming off your skin can make you smell like an old dosser.
- When you get to work keep a low profile, a lack of sleep can sometimes make one overexcitable and prone to talk a lot.

Girly knicker tip
If you haven't any fresh spare pants, flip the ones you're wearing over and wear them sunny-side-down.

I'm worried I'll embarrass myself in a posh restaurant

- Don't be tempted to drink too much if you're nervous. If you keep reaching for your glass, ask for some water and gulp that instead.

- If you're not sure what to do with the food or cutlery, follow the others' lead. If they don't know either have a laugh about it.

- If you have to choose the wine, don't be shy of asking for the waiter's suggestions. When you are offered some to taste, *do* taste it — you'll soon realise if it's corked due to a funny smell and musty taste. They don't offer it to see if you like the wine!

Girly dignity and the demon drink

How to retain your dignity when you're seriously pissed:

- Refuse any offers of joined-up dancing — you won't be able to stay on your feet.
- Don't start smoking fags if you don't usually — you'll look bloody ridiculous and an obvious beginner.
- Be extra careful about who you lurch towards to steady yourself — you might end up having to defend yourself from your rescuer.
- Keep your mouth shut if it's a work do and your boss is nearby.

Hangovers – all there is to know

Even with the best intentions in the world, most of us end up
with a hangover after a really good night out – the going-too-
far when you know you shouldn't (oh *go on*, one more's not
going to make any difference now, anyway) and that morning-
after feeling of exhaustion, slight hysteria and weird cravings.
And that's just your essential organs crying out for help,
never mind what else you got up to.

Because it's a serious business we feel we should devote
ample space to this aspect of our lives, so put your feet up,
pour yourself a drink, and read carefully …

The girly guide to try to avoid – and then survive – a hangover

Many of you will know the golden rules, but let's face it, do you obey them? Here is our tried and tested guide, in three easy stages ...

Stage 1 – before and during ...

- The old wives' tale of lining the stomach beforehand. Milk is usually the best for this but some even swear by drinking olive oil to prevent alcohol absorption by the stomach – but we agree this doesn't sound too attractive an option, even more vomit-inducing than a hangover.

- Alternate alcohol with glasses of water – or at least juices or soft drinks if you really hate water.

- If you want to stop drinking but are worried about appearing a wuss, get a mineral water with ice and lemon and pretend it's a gin and tonic.

- Drinks with bubbles (ah champagne!) are more speedily absorbed so watch out.

- Nibbling while drinking slows down alcohol absorption.

- Cocktails are good to kick off with because the fruit juices they contain (cranberry, strawberry, orange) help your body to recover from dehyration and vitamin deficiencies, *really ...*

- Be careful of sea breezes: when grapefruit juice is combined with alcohol it increases its toxicity.

Stage 2 – after …

When you've stopped spinning around and belting out the chorus to 'I will survive' remember to take these measures.

❦ Drink at least a pint of water before hitting the sack.

❦ Take a globe artichoke herbal supplement. This may sound bizarre but we *promise* it really does work. A chemical in these tablets (available in chemists) helps the liver break down the alcohol, so easing the knock-on symptoms. But note, take tablets before indulging – as well as afterwards – for full preventative effects.

❦ Milkthistle is from the same family as artichoke so is also very good at cleansing the liver. Take before you go to bed.

❦ Sleep. The best hangover cure ever.

Stage 3 ... **help I've got the hangover from hell!**

OK, so you ignored the above, yet again, but have no fear, we've brought together some of our favourite tried and tested solutions to help get through the morning after. Of course not all hangovers are the same and sometimes things work for us and other times they don't ... keep this list to hand to pick 'n' mix the morning after.

> Water. Keep drinking lots of it. You know you should.

Girly guide to hangover beauty

If you can be fully confident of not compounding your feelings of despair the morning after by waking up with badly applied fake tan along with your puffy eyes, apply some fake tan to your face before you crash out — it takes that pale ghost-like look away and instead you'll have a deceptively healthy glow!

- Take a Nurofen with a can of coke. What a combo! The only way to shift that splitting headache and pick you up. Sugary drinks of any kind all help — and health goes out of the window during hangover hell.

- Cranberry juice. Very good for the kidneys which are the body's water-control system and work hard to rehydrate the body. Grapefruit juice is recommended for the liver — mix it with the cranberry for a virgin sea breeze.

- Herbal teas. Try to stick to these instead of coffee, which though seeming the only thing to kick-start the day actually makes your dehydration worse. Peppermint tea is great for the stomach — and helps the nausea — and by adding a bit of honey you might also ease your headache.

* Greasy fry-up. Yes, never mind all this herbal clap-trap, we all know that sometimes only this can hit the spot. Your body is demanding that carbohydrate and fat. Bacon sarnies during a post-mortem in the office canteen — what could be better?

* Healthy breakfast. Try a smoothie (p.117) or a poached or boiled egg on brown bread — good comfort foods which will help stabilise your blood sugar levels.

Girly hair of the dog

Bloody Mary. A cliché maybe, but it works, with that pick-me-up that only alcohol can give. In case you don't know, it's basically vodka, tomato juice, Worcester sauce, Tabasco, lemon juice and seasoning. And the tomato provides vitamins!

* Ginger.
Traditionally used for stomach complaints, ginger soothes after high alcohol consumption and is very good to lessen horrible waves of nausea. Try ginger tea or chew on crystallised ginger (this also helps those sugar cravings).

* Over the counter remedies.
Resolve and Berocca they're fab. Stock up for the Christmas party season.

* Teabags or eyemasks.
Keep one of those gel-filled eyemasks in the fridge at all times — it really does help revitalise the head and eyes. Teabags, boiled, then chilled and laid on the eyes also help to sooth puffy and bloodshot eyes.

- Smoothies. Very good to soothe the stomach, rehydrate and provide that essential sugar injection. Throw bananas – which contain magnesium (said to be good for a lager hangover!) – milk, yoghurt, any fruits you've got, into a blender. Add honey to sweeten – also good for its cleansing abilities.

- Egg yolks or 'Prairie Oysters' (a raw egg, seasoned and swallowed whole) – add to smoothies or a Bloody Mary. Yuk, yes another cliché but they contain choline (and cysteine which destroys free radicals) which, like artichoke, helps the liver break down alcohol.

Girly morning after cocktail

Fling 1tbs honey, then banana, kiwi fruit, pineapple into blender. Add yoghurt, whizz and drink.

- Hot shower. A really powerful hot shower is great, especially if you direct the nozzle to the back of the neck. The theory is that this will relax the tense muscles in your neck and give relief from your headache.

- Aromatherapy bath. Add about 5 drops of an essential oil to a very warm bath. The wafting fragrances will do wonders. Lavender, juniper, fennel and ginger oils are all good. Eucalyptus will clear your head and toxins from your body, Peppermint revitalises by stimulating circulation. Sandalwood soothes.

Bouncing back from a big night out

❧ Pamper yourself for the day if your hangover coincides
with the weekend — or have an impromptu 'duvet day'!
Soak yourself in a warm tub, or the aromatherapy bath.
Cleanse your face — exfoliate and body-brush to get that
blood flowing, relax with a facepack.

❧ Reviving facepack. Now available in handy sachets in
chemists. Full of zingy, resfreshing and soothing
ingredients to wake your skin up and get blood to the outer
layers again. They are especially good when kept in the
fridge. Or make your own facial (see pp.74–76).

- Exercise! Some people swear by a good work-out the morning after to sweat out all those toxins, but most of us mortals have problems getting out of the front door. A brisk stroll to work really does help by getting more oxygen into the blood, which flows more quickly to the liver and speeds up the rescue operation.

- Sex. There's nothing better than a horizontal morning workout to brighten your morning, and get the blood pumping to increase your metabolic rate, which means your liver will work faster to rid you of your hangover symptoms.

Literary girly

As Kingsley Amis famously wrote in his book, *On Drink*:
'There's no better cure than making love to your partner the following morning.'

- Comfort-dress. Slip into something both slinky, soft and comforting, avoid red and black as they can be a bit harsh against a pale, washed-out complexion.

- Face rescue. Try our homemade remedies for red eyes, puffy eyes, dark shadows (see pp.65 and 69), or instant pick-me-up face pack (p.74). We swear by keeping an eyemask in the fridge and using one of those instant radiance products from Boots, Clarins or Estée Lauder.

- Make-up. Use tinted moisturiser to give you some colour. Don't try anything too fiddly — a bad attack of the shakes and a tube of liquid eyeliner just don't bode well. Keep things simple.

- Do something to make you feel better — spend some money, have a nice lunch to dissect the night before with a mate.

- Appropriate behaviour. Be on your guard when in the fragile, vulnerable state that is a hangover. You can say the wrong things, forget stuff, press the wrong button when sending an email, call your lover by the wrong name … these are all things that can compound your hangover hell.

Boosting your immune system to survive the party season

- Make sure you get lots of Vitamin C. This comes in berry fruits, fresh green and red peppers, but also citrus fruits so keep drinking the orange juice, the virgin sea breezes …
- Take supplements of Vitamin E, selenium and zinc.
- Garlic – a great anti-viral agent that can be taken in daily, odourless tablets.
- Ginseng and B vitamins – very good combo for fighting party-season burnout and other periods of protracted stress!

Sexy, healthy girly stuff

Men love them, but stockings aren't just for getting men in the mood:

- They're not only sexier they're more economical; buy two pairs of the same stockings, if you get a ladder in one leg just throw it away, and keep on using the other three legs.

- They can help prevent thrush and cystitis as your girly bits stay cooler than in tights.

And
- An oldie but a goodie – use clear nail polish to stop runs in stockings and tights.

Staying In

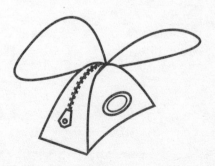

make it look like you've been cooking for hours.

I've got people coming for dinner in 30 minutes and the place is a mess

You've finally got rid of your flatmates for the night but now you need help!

- Spray furniture polish near the front door. The heady aroma creates the illusion that you've spent all day with your sleeves rolled up. Empty all visible bins. Do something creative with your throw cushions – like plump them up!

- Open a can of Coke – have a slurp and pour the rest down the loo to dissolve yukky stains. Flush just before guests arrive. Check bathroom for embarrassing objects left around …

- Put a smear of flour or sauce on your face and clothes to make it look like you've been cooking for hours.

- Get a box and clear away all unnecessary stuff from surfaces — hide it in cupboard. But leave out the odd cooking gadget (blender, lemon squeezer) for effect.

- Fill the sink and throw in the dirty dishes or, if you really don't have time, put them in a bag and hide it in the cupboard.

- Remember to remove any knickers or stockings drying on radiators. Or undies wedged under the sofa, etc …

- Set the table — it diverts attention from everything else — put out napkins, candles and wine glasses.

- Last but not least, hide a multitude of sins by turning off all the lights and light scented candles instead.

When they arrive

Give them a strong drink and some crisps and dips immediately and make them comfortable in the tidiest part of the flat or house, while you start 'cooking' your homemade meal. Pour yourself a drink and relax — the worst is over.

Girly homemade tricks

- To cunningly deceive, transform your ready-made dips into the 'homemade' variety by scraping into bowls and sprinkling chopped fresh herbs over the top - try parsley or chives.

- Transform shop-bought desserts into ones that look as if you've made them yourself. If for example you've bought a chocolate torte, bash it about a bit so it appears less perfect, dust with cocoa powder or icing sugar so plate is also sprinkled. Add fresh strawberries; smear chocolate about your person.

Girly tips for appearing to be the perfect hostess

You don't want to waste precious time cooking when you could be making yourself gorgeous or drinking and flirting with your guests. Here's how to cheat your way to culinary success:

- Always have enough booze in — start with a nice bottle of wine when they arrive and will notice it more, then move on to the cheaper stuff and then the very-cheap-and-nasty when everyone's too blitzed to notice.

- Having a ready-mixed jug of a cocktail is often a good way to kick off and avoids the panic of trying to make lots of different drinks at once — and small details such as using fresh mint in Pimm's, or lemon in your vodka and tonic, makes it look like you've put in some effort.

- Always have plenty of nibbles (plus cheeses and nice bread) and salami from the deli, olives and nuts for while you're preparing — or in case main course goes wrong.

- Don't go for the most popular M&S dishes — your canny ready-meal consuming mates will recognise them straight away. Try the other supermarkets or Italian delis where you can buy 'home-cooked' pasta dishes and sauces.

- Have a quick look at the ingredients on the packets so you know how to bluff when asked 'what's in this then?'

Girly punch

A killer punch made from a cheap bottle of vodka, fruit juices and lemonade, adding lumps of fruit and ice cubes, is a good way to start things going with a swing without spending too much dosh.

- Get some fresh herbs, chop and sprinkle over food after you've plated up – this makes even ready meals look homemade.

- Don't go for anything too complicated or that you haven't tried before. Stick to simple things – with good fresh ingredients – rather than trying to recreate what you had at a restaurant last week.

Top girly housekeeping tips

Help, I've just put a huge scratch in someone's coffee table ...

- Find a brown crayon, melt a little with a cigarette lighter and rub it into the scratch. If you can't find a crayon try a little a little bit of shoe polish the right colour. It should disguise the mark so you won't have to own up.

- If you scorch your clothing, try soaking it overnight in some full-fat milk — it is something unexplainable (to us) to do with enzymes in the milk — but it works.

Bicarbonate of soda is a girly essential:
- Dissolve in a little water and apply to skin to ease bee stings.
- A tablespoonful in the washing machine takes any odour out of your washing — great for pongy wet washing that has been left in the machine for days.
- A teaspoonful dissolved in water will make your pee more alkaline and stop the burning if you have cystitis.
- Sprinkle a little in your boyfriend's or your own trainers overnight to absorb stinkiness.

I've had a mad time lately – too much booze and late nights …

You can rejuvenate yourself in a weekend by staying in and:

- switching off the phone
- wearing your comfiest slouching around clothes
- drinking bucketfuls of water to flush out the toxins
- catching up on sleep
- leaving off your make-up, putting on a face mask and pampering yourself with essential oil baths
- mini detox by laying off the booze and cigarettes – you can do it for a weekend …
- eating lots of fruit and veg
- going for a gentle walk in the park to get some fresh air.

I just dashed to the corner shop in my worst trackie with dirty hair and bumped into the man I adore

Don't worry about it — just make sure it never happens again!

- First take steps to ensure you'll bump into him again, this time looking like the ultimate sex goddess.
- Second go through your casual clothes and chuck out any frumpy clothes that make you look like a bag lady.
- Next time you buy slobbing-out clothes make sure they look good too, even tracksuits can be flattering if you get the right shape.
  - Wear a strappy vest with your tracks and if your breasts are firm go without a bra, you'll be comfy but look sexy.
  - If you must do oversized, make it the cardi over a top which shows off your shape. Unzip if you spot anyone you want to impress.

Playing
Away

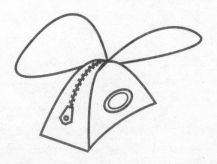

Girly guide to holiday fun

Despite being bombarded with beach-body diet plans in every glossy magazine from the beginning of Spring, most of us never quite get around to that pre-holiday diet, extra gym sessions or all-over-body fake tan. So whether you've got a week to go, or perhaps only a day, we offer the essential girly guide to whipping that body into the best possible shape in a very short space of time – to get you looking like a natural-born beach babe every minute of your holiday.

Holiday countdown

If you've got only a week or two to go before you squeeze into that teeny bikini, don't worry, there's still sufficient time to make a difference. Rather than go on a starvation diet that will leave you weak and vulnerable at a time when you need to be shoring up your body's defences, cut down on portion sizes and 'bad' foods. Forget the cakes, biscuits, crisps and late-night takeaways. Up the salads, fresh fruit and vegetables. Try to cut back on your alcohol intake — and step up the gym visits if you can. Even a few daily sit-ups will help. Body-brushing your thighs and buttocks in the shower every morning for a week will definitely enhance their appearance.

24-hour bikini emergency

Whether you're lucky enough to find out that your new man is whisking you away to Sardinia for a surprise weekend, or you just haven't got round to organising yourself, and you've now only got a day before you get on that flight. Here is a quick girly guide to covering all bases.

Check ...

> Have you faked it? Tanned wobbly bits look a lot better than white ones, never mind how horrific it is to be the whitest person on the beach.

> Have you defuzzed? Sort out that bikini line ...

> Are your feet an embarrassment? (see p 81)

> Worried about that convex stomach? (see p 102)

Fake tanning disasters to avoid

There are now many different types of fake tan — creams, gels, mousses, sprays and even moist wipes. The tinted variety is often better so you can see where you've applied it — and gives you instant colour. There are also different types especially suited for the face which may have extra moisturiser and be unscented. Check whether they contain an SPF of at least 15 — essential if you're going to be out in the (real) sun. Match to your skin tone — they come in light, medium and dark shades.

Girly embarrassment dodging tip

Water-test your bikini in the shower — it may be see-through when wet. It may be better to avoid flimsy white bikinis for this reason … unless of course you go for the full Brazilian.

Girly tanning tips:

- Mix with moisturiser for problem areas where skin is drier or creased — ankles, backs of knees, toes and between fingers. Watch out for inner arms too.
- Don't apply it immediately after shower or it won't absorb properly. If you've got extra time, apply a second layer to intensify the colour.
- A common mistake is actually applying too little so be confident if you've done the right prep of exfoliating and moisturising.
- Be careful of letting it dry before you don light-coloured — wash hands, especially your cuticles which absorb colour.
- Take fake tan with you on holiday to top up before you get a genuine bronze. Decant into handy travel-size — and unidentifiable — pot.

Girly beach body tips

- Flat stomach — avoid salty foods, caffeine and alcohol which cause water retention. (See pp.103–105 for more tips.)

- Hair — try to have a trim before you go to lose all the split ends. Protect by covering up with a scarf or hat or with special sprays (or even suntan lotion in an emergency). Make sure you're extra careful if you've got bleached hair.

- Bikini line — go for warm-wax roll-on types or cream hair removers if you haven't had time to go for a professional job. Try to do a day before you go so follicles can calm down — and before you self-tan.

- Speedy pedicure — if you have time on your side then a chiropodist can give your toes a good going-over, but otherwise try the bare minimum: clip nails, tidy cuticles, get rid of lumps of hard skin, soak or slather in rich oil/moisturiser. Then after letting this soak in, apply a coat of clear nail varnish; or bright colours if you want to draw attention to your toes. Your feet will look instantly better.

Hot tips for looking like a beach babe in your bikini and not a beached whale

- Go for a size up rather than one that will be biting into you and reveal slight bulges on your back or buttocks.

- Make sure you try bending down, sitting and stretching when you try one on or you may be in for a big shock on the beach. This even applies to you skinnies.

Desperate to look flat-bellied?
Hold stomach in for the entire holiday, keep your shoulders back and head up, lie on your back , propped up on your elbows – hold this position until it is time for lunch, eat like a horse, everyone's seen your gorgeous belly by now – wear your sarong after lunch.

- That push-up number may be great in a changing room but once it's wet and you bend down to adjust your towel, oops, your boobs have brimmed over and nearly fallen out completely.

- You don't have to stick to 'slimming black' — bright colours can flatter just as much, and patterns like polka dots keep the eye moving around and away from your figure.

- Go for bright, fun and stylish accessories such as a bandana, trendy bangles, big shades or girly flip-flops to make you feel good and look cool. Think curvy, glamorous filmstar look.

Desperate beach tip
No time for waxing, fake tan or dieting? — bury yourself in the sand or buy a king-size sarong.

Girly holiday essentials kit

- Aloe vera gel is wonderfully soothing for sunburnt skin or bites or stings — available from chemists.

- Essential oils — citronella, lavender and tea tree deter insects.

- Multivitamin tablets — especially good if you suffer stomach upsets so you can replace lost nutrients, and your immune system is helped by vitamins C, E and A.

- Anti-diarrhoea tablets.

- Cranberry extract tablets for holiday doses of cystitis — Watch out! all that extra sex and dehydration makes it worth taking provisions if you are prone to it (see p.172)

- Emergency first-aid kit. Pack separately from toiletries in case of spillages. Remember to pack this or any medicines in hand luggage.

- If you are travelling with a companion, pack half your stuff in each case — if one goes astray you at least have some clothes to wear, rather than trying to fit into your best mate's size 8 bikini — or if it's your boyfriend …

- Take a long-sleeved shirt or top to cover up if you get burnt — or to protect from mozzie bites in the evenings.

How to survive a long-haul flight and look fabulous

Your carry-on girly kit

- Vaseline
- rosewater or evian spray – mist your face regularly to prevent your skin from dehydrating
- lavender oil – dab on yourself, the pillow …
- moisturiser to reapply regularly
- mints for fresh breath
- hair ties
- herbal sleeping pills if the flight is long enough to sleep
- keep off the fizzy drinks, even the seemingly harmless mineral water
- panty liners to keep pants fresh
- magazines, books, Walkman

* a bottle of water — you can never get enough from the cabin crew
* blow-up pillow
* eyeshield
* earplugs
* Rescue Remedy — for fearful flyers, use few drops under your tongue.

Dress in comfortable layers. Tight trousers can be hell. Wear comfortable shoes as feet swell. A pashmina can double as a blanket or something to put under your head on the flight.

Girly jetlag tip

Siberian ginseng will increase your body's ability to fight fatigue. Take every day for week before flight to try to combat worst symptoms of jetlag.

I'm scared of getting DVT (deep vein thrombosis)

Now known to be a much more serious risk to long-haul travellers than previously realised. Women on the pill are especially at risk, but also those that have had recent surgery or illness — or a history of blood-clotting problems.

Tips:

- Keep moving around in your seat. Stretch legs and toes.

- Move out of your seat as much as possible — aisle seats better for this.

- Drink plenty of water — rather than too much alcohol or caffeine.

- Take an aspirin or a more natural alternative – pine bark supplement, also known as Pycnogenol. This can be taken in week or so leading up to flight as preparation. Available from healthfood shops.

- Buy and wear support tights as they encourage good blood circulation. The Aviation Health Authority have developed special compression socks if you don't want to wear tights.

Girly eye protection

if you get sore eyes spray Evian/rosewater on cotton pads and lay on eyes. Wear glasses instead of contact lenses which become dry. You can always put lenses in just before you land.

Make yourself beautiful while on the beach

◊ Emulate Geri Halliwell or Madonna. Do some stretching exercises or yoga. N.B. only to be done when boyfriend is snoozing after lunch – otherwise his derisory hoots of laughter will have the whole beach watching.

◊ Don't worry that you look a complete prat – nobody knows you. If you really don't want to be seen, do some water aerobics in the sea – submerged running on the spot will tone up your legs.

> **Girly no-burn tip**
> Spread your lipbalm or sunstick down your hairline to avoid burning your scalp.

- Use the sand to exfoliate yourself. Rub it all over.

- Rub that suntan lotion into your toe-nails and finger-nails. Your cuticles will be conditioning and nails growing faster while you lie there tanning. At the end of two weeks you'll have much better-looking nails.

- Bored of reading or just lying in the sun? Give yourself a quick manicure – it'll save time later when you're getting ready to go out.

Girly looking hot survival tip
Take 2 bikinis or swimsuits – one for when other the one is drying off. Also, if you only had one and you lost it, you might have to spend the rest of the week in a naff and ill-fitting one from the local shops.

How to look like a sun-kissed beach babe in 5 minutes

After a day on the beach, jump in the shower, slather yourself in luxuriously, fragranced shower gel, douse your hair with a good deep conditioner. After the shower, slap on some body lotion, spray your limbs with one of those light, oily, sheeny sprays, before slipping on that strappy dress and a pair of sandals. Put on a bit of lipgloss, mascara and light bronzing powder and you're away.

Girly packing tip
If you're short of space, why not decant suntan lotion into a small tub. Film roll canisters are ideal because they have very good seals so you can slip one into handbag or pockets. Chuck away when it's going-home time.

How to survive a full-on clubbing destinaton:

If you're off somewhere like Ibiza or Ayia Napa or Magaluf try to pace yourself on the alcohol front. Hot temps will make dehydration worse so don't go to sleep on the beach after a big night unless you're in the shade – it'll take you days to recover from the headache when you wake up.

- Eat regularly, even if not proper sit-down meals.

- Drink lots of water – if you don't find this easy, remember watermelon is 90% water so nibble on chunks of this. It is also great for the immune system.

- Try to give your body – especially your liver – a night off at least once or twice. You'll be less likely to get run down.

- Don't mix drinks and drugs.

- Don't overdo the sun. Use sunscreen with a high enough protection factor. Build up gradually. Remember it washes off in water so needs to be reapplied every hour or so.

- Avoid stomach upsets by drinking bottled water and watching what you eat — remember ice cubes are often made from tap water. Make sure you always have some bottled water in your room — especially if you've been drinking heavily.

Lazy girly tip

To 'iron' your clothes while you're on hols, hang them up the night before you want to wear them and splash, flick or spray water onto the creases. The weight of the water makes most crumples fall out by the next day.

Sex on the beach

Girly guide to holiday sex

- If you're on the pill, remember to take enough supplies to last you the whole trip — a spare packet in your handbag is a good idea in case your luggage gets lost or stolen.

- Remember you may want to run on packs to avoid having to deal with your period on holiday. Check on the packet instructions or with your GP about how and if you can do this correctly with your particular type of pill.

- It's not pure chance that too many of us get pregnant on holiday. It's not just the extra bonking but also that it's easy to forget that stomach upsets or sickness mean that you won't have digested your pill properly. Take condoms to use for the next few days to be extra sure of being safe.

- Take condoms — even if you are on the pill — they also protect against STDs. It's easier — and probably cheaper — to buy them at home first as in some countries they can be hard to find or of poor quality (check for the kite mark!). Keeping a couple in your pocket or purse doesn't mean you're a slut — just canny. It could mean the difference between a holiday romance and not having it ...

- Did the condom split? Think you might be pregnant? You can get the morning-after pill in many places — over the counter in Spain but also from a GP, family planning clinic or hospital. (Check with your holiday rep about the location of these.)

Beware of spiked drinks

We've all read about Rohypnol, and whilst it is still generally quite rare it's wise to be on your guard on a night out, especially in unfamiliar surroundings. It is better if you see the barman serve your drink, so beware of drinks bought by strangers from the bar, or leaving your drink unattended. Only accept drinks from people you trust. If you think your drink tastes a bit odd or you begin to feel strangely drunk, stop drinking and remove yourself from the situation, with a friend if possible.

Essential girly website
Many holiday resorts or backpacker destinations have internet cafés now. Use the net to search for help finding the morning-after pill locally. Not-2-late.com — an emergency contraception website where you can search for nearest place to go.

Girly guide to common-sense safety for girls travelling alone abroad

- Make sure you stay in a street that has bars and late-night shops where there are plenty of people around. It's wise not to walk home alone to your hotel after dark. Be wary of people overhearing your room number if you collect your key from the reception desk.

- Watch out for pickpockets. Be especially careful in crowded places or streets, or on the metro. If you're jostled or distracted by someone it's often a decoy. Make sure the type of bag you use is secure – ones with open tops can easily be 'dipped'.

- Don't carry huge amounts of cash around — or carry all your cash cards together. Hide in separate places in your luggage.

- Keep the lost-or-stolen phone number for your bank cards to hand — not in the purse! — so you can cancel immediately if it gets stolen. Might be useful to keep copies of the numbers somewhere else in your luggage.

Girly holiday dos
- Money — don't carry large amounts on you — and divide up what you have amongst luggage in case pick-pocketed or theft of baggage.
- Take spare pack of contact lenses, prescription glasses or essential medication.

- Get insurance. This is not just for thefts of valuables but also for delays of luggage and health problems. Check small print for the extent of cover – and make sure you get a police incident report/crime number if you suffer theft or mugging or policy won't be valid. Take the insurance company helpline number with you.

- Find out the country's number for emergency police. Put it in your mobile phone speed-dial just in case.

- Loss of passport? Check with rep/holiday guide where the nearest British Consulate or High Commission is. They can also arrange medical attention or help in case of assault.

Health

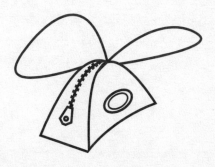

Eating to avoid health emergencies

Sometimes you get to the end of a week and realise all you've eaten since last weekend is junk food. Life is so hectic, and its easy to forget to eat properly. This checklist will help you to stay on track by reminding you what you should be eating to stay healthy. Make a list and stick it on your fridge so that you keep an eye on your eating as you reach for another glass of wine.

Every day:

» live yoghurt - provides 'good' bacteria for your stomach
» 2 pieces of fruit
» fresh vegetables
» 6 glasses of still water to keep you and your skin hydrated
» a cup of green tea – a great anti-oxidant (keep it at work and remember to drink it)
» wholegrain bread - for fibre.

At least once a week:
- oily fish – sardines, mackerel and salmon
- non-oily fish – cod, hake, haddock
- unsalted nuts – pistachios, cashews
- garlic and onions
- chilli
- green and yellow fruit and veg – melon, corn, peppers, peas
- dried fruit – apricots, sultanas, figs or prunes

Girly get-your-veg-in tip
Grab a bag of pre-cut veg and some houmous from the supermarket and eat when you're having a drink – it'll soak up the booze a bit and make sure you get your veg at the same time.

If you must – not very often, definitely not more than once a week:

- chocolate – make it dark chocolate and organic to feel more saintly while you're being naughty
- cake, croissants, biscuits
- fizzy mineral water
- fried food
- 'diet drinks' – artificial sweeteners are a health hazard
- take-aways – They're high in saturated fat or chemical flavourings. It's better to make your own stir-frys or curries.

Girly supplements

Girly essentials like cigarettes, alcohol and coffee all deplete your body of Vitamin C, so get yourself an extremely good supplement if you are frequently out on the lash.

I desperately need to lose weight but I love grazing ...

Having lots of the right snacks on hand is the number one secret. Firsty, don't have anything in your cupboards or fridge that will blow your resolve to lose weight, and secondly, keep loads of healthy snacks on hand so that you're not tempted to run out to the shops for a packet of crisps or some chocolate.

Keep in the cupboard:

- dried fruit is really sweet – try bananas, apricots, pears, figs and prunes
- rice cakes or Ryvita to be topped with avocado or low-fat houmous or cream cheese
- mixed fresh nuts
- chilli olives
- pumpkin seeds

Or try this frozen girly treat:
Our favourite is so low-fat it's unbelievable. All you need is
low-fat plain yoghurt and some fruit: peaches, nectarines,
berries in summer, bananas in winter. Push the fruit through a
sieve with a wooden spoon (the banana you can just mash up),
add the fruit pulp to yoghurt, stir in and freeze. You could buy
some groovy ice-lolly holders and make little ice-lollies.

Don't totally deprive yourself – promise yourself a
chocolate bar or a huge bun but only once a week. Make it a
regular day so you can look forward to it.

If you fail – Don't worry, chocolate may contain a lot of
calories but it is good for you too. Its high levels of antioxidant
flavoroids help to stop arteries clogging. And remember the
darker the better.

Help, I keep getting cystitis what can I do …

Cystitis can be caused by an overdose of vigorous sex (hence it's name honeymoonitis), but also increased by the number of sexual partners and can lead to kidney infections. It is important to seek treatment for it quickly.

Symptoms to watch out for are having to go to the loo very frequently – and only passing a few drops – and a burning feeling when you go. You might get kidney pains in the lower back too.

Do's

> Drink plenty of water.

> Drink cranberry juice or take cranberry extract tablets – available from healthfood shops.

* Moderate alcohol intake as much as possible. Also try to cut down on citrus fruits and caffeine which dehydrate.

* Wear cotton undies as nylons increase likelihood of bacterial infections.

* Wear stockings not tights!

* Go to the loo as soon as possible after sex – urine works as a flush.

* Mix a teaspoon of bicarbonate of soda with some water, it will make your pee alkaline and it won't burn as much.

How to cope with an 'abnormal' smear test result

Don't panic, it is more common than you think – 1 in 12 is abnormal, but it is essential that you make an appointment with your doctor who will advise you of the next step – whether treatment is necessary or not. If you want a second opinion, or to get more information, go to a sexual health clinic – they do smear tests all the time so they are usually more experienced than your local surgery.

It is even more important to have regular smear tests if you:
- smoke
- have a lot of sexual partners
- lost your virginity under age 20.

But the most important risk factor for cervical cancer is ... not having a smear test.

Girly guide to the dreaded thrush

Few of us have avoided this irritating problem, often caused by taking too many antibiotics which kill our natural immune system. There are creams easily available at the chemist and there is also natural yoghur to use in the same way as thrush cream, but also:

- take acidophilus tablets or eat live yoghurts regularly
- steer clear of yeast-based or fermented foods (alcohol, cheeses, mushrooms, vinegar and pickles, white bread)
- avoid nylon underwear and 'intimate' toiletries like vaginal sprays or powders
- a soak in a warm salt bath is soothing (add 5tbs salt to bath).

Help I suffer from bloating and wind …

It's so embarrassing – I don't want to fart in front of my bloke!

Here's how to have near-perfect digestion

- Take a probiotic supplement to help improve your system – especially important to take after you've been using antibiotics (see your health food store).
- Eat live yoghurt everyday — it must say live on the packaging.
- Avoid sugar and refined flour products like pasta and white bread.
- Eat more food to help your digestion such as bananas, honey, tomatoes, leeks, asparagus, garlic and onions.
- Chew your food properly, don't gulp.

Vitamins

Most of us don't always eat all the foods to get the right amounts of vitamins and minerals, so taking a supplement or two really does help. Not only do you decrease your chances of getting ill – but they help boost your body during times when you are run down and vulnerable. If you take nothing else, a simple multivitamin and mineral tablet with breakfast is a good start. See p.122 for the girly guide to boosting your immune system during the party season.

Other useful vitamin, mineral and herbal supplements:

- Oil of evening primose – for PMT
- Ginseng – for energy, emotional and mental balance
- Fish oils – great for menstrual pains and will ward off osteoporosis

- Zinc – if you're prone to spots or IBS – or for pill-users
- Selenium – an antioxidant, great for the immune system but also for a healthy mental and emotional balance
- Vitamin E – for your immune system and for skin (see p.68)
- Vitamin C – for smokers, and if you feel you're coming down with a cold as it is great for the immune system
- Vitamin B Complex – great for stress, and B6 for hormonal balance.

Girly vitamin tip

Take your vitamin supplements in the morning. They may overstimulate you and prevent you sleeping if you take them at night.

Then again … if you're planning a romp with your man, then go for it!

I go really wild with rage before my period – how can I keep my hormones under control?

Hormones have a huge influence on your physical, mental and emotional wellbeing. It is tempting to curl up on the sofa with a chocolate bar and avoid exercise just before and during your period. Don't force yourself to the gym but try to do a little gentle exercise – it will actually make you feel better. Put the telly on, throw a big cushion on the floor and do some simple stretches. See the lazy girl's exercise tips on p.182.

Don't eat your broccoli

I bet you thought you'd never be told to leave your greens. Broccoli and sprouts contain oestrogen which you don't need more of in the days before your period.

Comfort yourself

While you're on the sofa feeling sorry for yourself, nibble on some pumpkin seeds and eat a banana. Or make yourself a huge avocado and cheese sarnie. These foods will elevate your serotonin levels which make you calmer and happier.

If you've got cramps …

Boost your endorphins — your body's natural painkiller — they help to reduce pain and create euphoria. Jogging or aerobics will help if you feel up to it, but its more likely you'll want to stay on the sofa — so eat Vitamin C-rich foods like oranges, kiwi fruit, strawberries and rosehip tea.

Can't cope, gotta have coffee/chocolate

Make your morning fix of cappucino a decaf before and during your period. If you really must have chocolate, make it a good quality one with a high-cocoa content, and enjoy it.

Emergency teas for the cupboard

Peppermint Calming for upset stomachs — indigestion, headaches and tension can all be alleviated with this simple tea. Also can be used as an emergency mouthwash.

Camomile Stress, anxiety, insomnia, stomach troubles, also for cystitis.

Lemon balm Anxiety, indigestion, mild depression and irritability and a mouthwash for toothache.

Nettle Excellent for the skin — so good to have on hand if you're having a few eruptions.

Green tea High in antioxidants, it also stimulates beneficial gut bacteria, which keeps your digestion working well.

Lazy girl's exercise

We never, ever exercise unless it's in front of the telly or incidental, like walking to the pub for a pint.

> Put a cushion between your knees — squeeze and hold for a count of 10, release, repeat as many times as you can.

> An afternoon walking around the shops can also pass as exercise, if you walk fast between shops and go to a lot of shops!

> At the bus stop or tube station, always use the wasted time to do buttock clenches.

Sometimes I worry about the effect of all those vodkas and Red Bulls and white wines ...

The liver is your detox organ: it is responsible for dealing with and eliminating toxins but we heap demands on it by drinking and eating sugary and fatty foods. If you've been boozing a lot make your liver's job a bit easier by eating foods that are easy to digest and process.

If you don't look after your liver you will be more prone to infections, and those colds and flus that go on for weeks, taking forever to shake off.

Fruits for the liver

Stock up when you know you're going to have a
heavy weekend and make a giant fruit salad using any
of the following:

apricots	lemons
avocados	oranges
bananas	papayas
berries	pineapples
cranberries	watermelons
grapefruit	

Did you know?

An unbalanced liver could be the cause of mood swings, allergies,
food sensitivities, fluid retention, candida and energy lows.

How to be a sensible girly and look after your health

- Check your breasts every month just after your period – your doctor can show you how. See a doctor straight away if you have any worries.

- If you think you've got any infections down below, get it checked out straight away.

- Keep up-to-date with your smear tests.

- Have a dental check-up every 6 months.

- Get any lumps or raised moles checked out a.s.a.p.

Serious girly moment ...

Sexually transmitted diseases (STDs) are on the rise. A recent report put the number of people with STDs as one in ten. If you have more than one sexual partner (lucky girl) it is especially wise to have regular checks as certain infections, such as chlamydia, can go unnoticed and leave you infertile. Many hospitals have a GU (genito-urinary) clinic where you can walk in and wait to see a doctor or nurse. All checks are confidential — and in some places you can book appointments rather than wait in line.

It's not just a girly thing

Make sure you get your partner checked out as well. It's all well and good for you to be tested and receive treatment for an STD — but not if he gives it back to you afterwards.

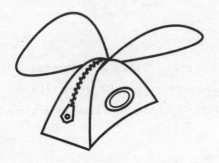

Look after yourself, above all have fun, and if you can't always be good at least take your vitamins, drink plenty of water, and always eat your greens.

Vermilion

Vermilion books are
available from all good
bookshops or by mail
from TBS Direct on:
01206 255 800.

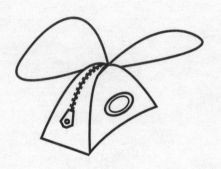